for
my grandmothers,
Mommylol & Lola Josie

my mom, Reina

my sister, Chantal

the women who inspired
me to chase my dreams

We Are Inspiring:
The stories of 32 inspirational
Asian American women

© 2019 Angel Trazo

PRINTED IN THE UNITED STATES OF AMERICA

www.ANGELTRAZO.com

ISBN 978-1-54397-416-4

ANNA MAY WONG
1905-1961

Anna May Wong (Wong Liu Tsong) was born on January 3, 1905 in Los Angeles, California. She grew up working in her father's laundry in Chinatown. After completing laundry deliveries, Anna used her tips to buy movie tickets. Watching movies inspired her to become an actress.

At first, her parents did not approve of her acting dreams, but Anna was unstoppable. She started as an extra, but soon began taking lead roles in American films. She was always cast as stereotypical Asian roles like the "China doll" or evil "dragon lady." This made her sad. Her father had always said, "We must be proud always of our people and our race." Nevertheless, she took these roles to help support her family.

In 1936, she traveled to China, where her parents now lived. There, Anna learned to love her Chinese heritage. She promised herself that she would "never play again in a film which shows the Chinese in an unsympathetic light."

Anna was the first Chinese American Hollywood movie star, as well as the first to gain international recognition. She acted for four decades in silent films, "talkies," and early television.

CHINESE AMERICAN ACTRESS

3

DR. CHIEN-SHIUNG WU
1912 -1997

Dr. Chien-Shiung Wu was born on May 31, 1912 in Liuhe, China. After reading the biography of two-time Nobel Prize winner, Marie Curie, as a teenager, Chien-Shiung dreamed of becoming a scientist. Little did she know, she would be nicknamed the "Chinese Madame Curie" and the "Queen of Nuclear Research." Though women were not encouraged to pursue education during her time, Chien-Shiung's parents disagreed. They advocated for the education of women and founded the the Ming De School for girls in China.

CHINESE AMERICAN
NUCLEAR PHYSICIST

4

Chien-Shiung attained her physics degree from the University of California, Berkeley. In 1944, she was invited to join the top-secret Manhattan Project. She is best known for her research that contradicted the hypothetical law of conservation of parity in nuclear physics. Though she did not win a Nobel Prize, her research built the foundation for her colleagues' win in 1957. She was awarded the second most prestigious physics award, the Wolf Prize, in 1978. Her colleagues would always say...

IF THE EXPERIMENT WAS DONE BY WU, IT MUST BE CORRECT

5

GRACE LEE BOGGS
1915-2015

Grace Yu Ping "Jade Peace" Lee Boggs was born on June 27, 1915 in Providence, Rhode Island above her father's Chinese restaurant. In 1940, she earned her PhD in Philosophy at Bryn Mawr. However, although she was a talented scholar, no university at the time would hire a Chinese American woman to teach ethics or political thought. So, Grace turned her passion toward civil rights activism. She married an African American auto worker and fellow activist, James Boggs, and moved to Detroit. Together, they fought for civil rights and the Black Power Movement.

CHINESE AMERICAN ACTIVIST, AUTHOR

YURI KOCHIYAMA
1921-2014

Yuri Kochiyama was born on May 19, 1921 in San Pedro, California to Japanese immigrant parents. She grew up like any other American girl, and described her twenty-year-old self as "a small-town gal living comfortably and totally apolitical." Then, on December 7, 1941, Japan bombed Pearl Harbor. Everything changed.

Yuri and her family were forced out of their home and incarcerated in a *concentration camp* (also known as "internment camps" or "relocation camps"), a plot of farmland and make-shift barn houses surrounded by barbed wire fences.

She went to Camp Jerome in Arkansas, one of ten concentration camps spread across the U.S. Yuri was one of 120,000 Americans and immigrants of Japanese ancestry who were detained.

JAPANESE AMERICAN ACTIVIST

BUILD BRIDGES, NOT WALLS

After WWII, Yuri moved to Harlem, New York, and spent her time at the Harlem Freedom School. *Freedom schools* teach the importance of learning about one's ethnic history and how to help one's community. In 1963, Yuri became good friends with human rights activist Malcom X. Together, they fought for the civil rights of Asian, black, and all Americans who felt marginalized.

PATSY MINK
1927 - 2002

Patsy Matsu Takemoto Mink was born on December 6, 1927 in Maui, Hawaii. Her parents are *Nisei* (KNEE-say) or second generation Japanese Americans, making Patsy a *Sansei* (SAHN-say) or third generation Japanese American. In 1948, Patsy completed her bachelor's degrees in zoology and chemistry from the University of Hawaii and dreamed of becoming a doctor. However, none of the medical schools she applied to would accept women. She thought that the best way to force medical schools to accept women would be through the judicial process.

So, she went to law school.

JAPANESE AMERICAN
LAWYER, POLITICIAN

Even after passing the Bar Exam, Patsy had trouble finding work as an attorney due to gender discrimination.

So, Patsy started her solo practice and became the first Japanese American woman to practice law in Hawaii. In 1964, she became the first Asian American woman (and the first woman of any ethnic minority) to be elected to the United States Congress where she served six consecutive terms (12 years). In 1970, she became the first Democratic woman to deliver a State of the Union response. Patsy spent her career fighting for her dreams, and in succeeding, she paved the way toward gender equity

SUGAR PIE DESANTO
1935

Umpeylia Marsema Balinton, "Queen of the West Coast Blues," was born to an African American mother and Filipino father on October 16, 1935. Though born in Brooklyn, New York, she grew up in San Francisco, California. She performed as Sugar Pie Desanto and became a famous female Blues, R&B, and Hip hop artist. Her showstopping performances featured not only her soulful vocals, but lively dancing and her legendary back flips. From 1959-1960, she performed at Harlem's legendary Apollo Theater with the "Godfather of Soul" himself, James Brown. She wrote over 100 songs and continues to perform today.

FILIPINA BLACK AMERICAN SINGER, MUSICIAN

NINOTCHKA ROSCA
1946

Ninotchka Rosca was born in 1946 in the Philippines before coming to the U.S. She refers to herself as a "transnational Filipina." In the Philippines, Ninotchka fought for civil rights and became a political prisoner for standing up against the dictatorial government of President Ferdinand Marcos. She was forced into exile in Hawaii, where she continued her work as a novelist, human rights activist, and feminist. She is currently an author and teacher based in New York City.

FILIPINA AMERICAN
AUTHOR, JOURNALIST, ACTIVIST

UERA WANG
1949

Vera Ellen Wang was born on June 27, 1949 in New York City to Chinese immigrant parents. Just after graduating from Sarah Lawrence College, she became the youngest editor at *Vogue Magazine*, where she stayed for 17 years.

Following *Vogue*, Vera joined the fashion brand *Ralph Lauren*, and later created her eponymous fashion house, *Vera Wang*, which specializes in bridal gowns. She has dressed celebrities like Michelle Kwan and Michelle Obama.

CHINESE AMERICAN FASHION DESIGNER

HELEN ZIA
1952

VINCENT CHIN

JUNE 23, 1982
DETROIT, MI

ASIAN AMERICAN DREAMS

CHINESE AMERICAN
JOURNALIST, ACTIVIST

Helen Zia was born to Chinese immigrant parents in Newark, New Jersey in 1952. She was one of the first women to graduate from Princeton University. She attended medical school at Tufts University in 1974, but left in 1976 to work as an autoworker in Detroit, Michigan. Her time in Detroit coincided with the downfall of the American auto industry and the murder of *Vincent Chin*, an innocent Chinese American man. Helen spread Vincent's story through journalism and activism, and her efforts helped galvanize Asian Americans to speak up against injustices. Throughout her lifetime, Helen has been a champion for the rights of Asian Americans, women, LGBTQ folks, and other marginalized communities. In 2008, Helen married her partner, Lia Shigemura. They were one of the first same-sex couples to wed in California.

WHO WAS Vincent Chin?

Vincent Jen Chin (1955-1982) was adopted from China by first generation Chinese American parents in 1961. He lived in Michigan his entire life and worked as an industrial draftsman. In the 1980's, the local auto industry was losing business due to the increasing popularity of Japanese export cars. This angered many who had worked in the American auto industry and led to anti-Asian hate crimes around Detroit. On the night of his bachelor party on June 19, 1982, Vincent and his friends were harassed by two white Chrysler autoworkers, Ronald Ebens and Michael Nitz. Ebens and Nitz, angry at Japan for "stealing their jobs," stalked Vincent out of the bar and beat him to death with a baseball bat. Neither Ebens nor Nitz spent any time in jail.

MAYA LIN
1959

CHINESE AMERICAN
ARCHITECT, ARTIST

Maya Ying Lin was born on October 5, 1959 in Athens, Ohio to immigrant parents. In 1981, when she was only 21 and a senior at Yale University, Maya's design was chosen out of 2,573 submissions as the winner for the Vietnam Veterans Memorial in Washington D.C. Her minimalist design was criticized for its lack of patriotic motifs; there were no men on horseback or American flags. Nevertheless, Maya's visionary monument moves the hearts of many. She designed an elegant pair of black granite walls inscribed with the names of the men and women who gave their lives during the Vietnam War. Maya creates "earthworks" that speak to the relationship between man-made objects and nature, and has also designed the Civil Rights Memorial in Alabama and the Museum of Chinese in America in New York. In 2009, she was awarded the National Medal of Arts by President Barack Obama.

TANI CANTIL-SAKAUYE
1959

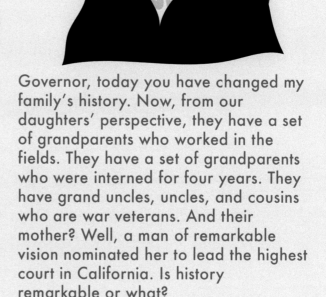

Tani Gorre Cantil was born on October 19, 1959 in Sacramento, California to a Filipino Portuguese father and Filipino mother. She currently serves as the 28th chief justice of the State of California, and is the first Filipina American and second woman to serve as the state's chief justice. After Gov. Arnold Schwarzenegger introduced her as a member of the CA Supreme Court on July 22, 2010, she replied,

Governor, today you have changed my family's history. Now, from our daughters' perspective, they have a set of grandparents who worked in the fields. They have a set of grandparents who were interned for four years. They have grand uncles, uncles, and cousins who are war veterans. And their mother? Well, a man of remarkable vision nominated her to lead the highest court in California. Is history remarkable or what?

FILIPINA PORTUGUESE AMERICAN
JUDGE, CHEIF JUSTICE OF CALIFORNIA

KAMALA HARRIS
1964

Kamala Harris was born on October 20, 1964 in Oakland, California to a Tamil Indian mother and Jamaican father. Growing up in Oakland, she had a stroller-eye view of the Civil Rights movement. In 2017, she was appointed to US Senator of California, making her the first South Asian American senator and only the second African American woman senator in history. She continues fighting for the rights of all communities in California.

INDIAN JAMAICAN AMERICAN U.S. SENATOR FROM CALIFORNIA

LUCY LIU
1968

Lucy Liu was born on December 2, 1968 in Queens, New York City to Chinese immigrants. She earned her bachelor's degree in Asian languages and cultures from the University of Michigan. At 21, she was discovered by a talent agent while riding the NY subway. Since, she has been an actress. Lucy is best known for her roles as Alex Munday in the film *Charlie's Angels* and Dr. Joan Watson in *Elementary*. Alongside acting, Liu has been a human rights advocate and served as an ambassador for the U.S. Fund for UNICEF. She is also a visual artist and raises her child, Rockwell, as a single mother.

CHINESE AMERICAN ACTRESS, ARTIST

MARGARET CHO
1968

Margaret Moran Cho was born on December 5, 1968 to Korean parents in San Francisco. Her father is a Korean joke book writer, and her mother defied an arranged marriage to marry him. A queer, Korean woman, Margaret's comedy acknowledges issues of family, race, gender, and other facets of her identity. She started writing comedy at 14 as a way to escape bullying. In 1994, she starred in and was the Executive Producer of *All-American Girl,* one of the first shows to feature an East Asian family. She is also a three-time Emmy and Grammy nominee.

KOREAN AMERICAN
COMEDIAN, ACTRESS

SOPHIA NTXAWM VUELO
1972

Sophia Nxtawm Vuelo was born in 1972 in Laos during wartime. Forty years ago, her family of eight left a refugee camp in Thailand to find sanctuary in the United States. They ended up in a Lutheran church in Eau Claire, Wisconsin, and has since called America home. "We didn't have a dime to our name... We truly were poorer than a church mouse," Sophia expressed. Despite this, she graduated with a degree in history from University of Minnesota, received her JD from Hamline University of Law, and became a lawyer with her own practice. She is the first Hmong American judge in the country and serves Minnesota.

don't let your birthplace or circumstances determine your DESTINY

HMONG AMERICAN JUDGE

THI BUI
1975

Thi Bui was born in Vietnam in 1975 and immigrated to the United States just three months before the end of the Vietnam War in 1978. Her family escaped to the United States as *boat people*, refugees who traveled by boat from Southeast Asia to America. Her graphic novel, *The Best We Could Do*, tells her mother's and father's family stories in Vietnam during the Fall of Saigon and is a National Bestseller. Thi also illustrated Bao Phi's children's book, *A Different Pond*. She currently works as a professor for the MFA in Comics at the California College of the Arts.

VIETNAMESE AMERICAN
ARTIST, AUTHOR, TEACHER 25

MINDY KALING
1979

Vera Mindy Chokalingam was born on June 27, 1979 in Cambridge, Massachusetts to a Tamil father and Bengali mother. At 24, Kaling joined *The Office* team as a writer/director and soon became full Executive Producer. In 2012, she produced and starred in *The Mindy Project*, a comedy series about Mindy Lahiri, an Indian American gynecologist living her best life in New York City. Since, she has continued acting in and producing film and television projects as well as writing books.

INDIAN AMERICAN
ACTRESS, COMEDIAN, PRODUCER

ALI WONG
1982

Alexandra "Ali" Dawn Wong was born on April 19, 1982 in San Francisco, California to a second generation Chinese American father and first generation Vietnamese American mother. She graduated from UCLA with a BA in Asian American Studies. At UCLA, she joined LCC Theatre Company (the largest and longest-running Asian American theatre company in the US). In 2011, *Variety* named her one of the "10 Comics to Watch," and her comedy shows, *Baby Cobra* and *Hard Knock Wife*, have been featured on Netflix. Ali is also a writer for the series *Fresh off the Boat* on ABC, a comedy about a Chinese American family.

CHINESE VIETNAMESE AMERICAN COMEDIAN, TV. SHOW WRITER

MICHELLE KWAN
1980

Michelle Wingshan Kwan was born on July 7, 1980 to Hong Kong immigrants in Torrance, California. At home, Michelle spoke a mix of Cantonese and English. She started skating at age five, inspired by her older brother and sister. However, paying for increased skating-rink time became a financial burden on her working class parents. At ten, her family could no longer afford lessons. Luckily, Michelle was offered financial assistance by a fellow member of the Los Angeles Figure Skating Club. Today, Michelle holds the all-time medal record for an American skater in any discipline – nine world medals (5 gold, 3 silver, and 1 bronze).

CHINESE AMERICAN FIGURE SKATER, OLYMPIAN

"My parents didn't have the means to provide brand-new skates, flashy costumes, or ice time. They were barely juggling multiple jobs, providing a roof over our heads, feeding us, working at the restaurant...My dad was working at a phone company, and they gave me this crazy opportunity to ice skate! Maybe I didn't get new skates, but I got used skates."

"I made it to the national championships in used skates that were custom-made for another girl. I still have those skates. Underneath the arch, there was a name crossed out and my dad had 'Michelle Kwan' written in."

29

EVA CHEN
1980

Eva Chen was born in 1980 and raised by immigrant parents in Greenwich Village, New York City. She became editor-in-chief of *Lucky Magazine* at age 33, making Eva the youngest editor to ever head a *Conde Nast* publication. She then worked at *Elle* in the beauty department before she became the Beauty and Health Director at *Teen Vogue*. Eva is currently Instagram's Head of Fashion Partnerships.

TAIWANESE AMERICAN
FASHION EDITOR

AIMEE SONG
1981

Aimee (rhymes with "Mommy") Song was born on September 3, 1981 in Los Angeles, California to immigrant parents. Aimee started her blog "Song of Style" in 2008. It was originally about interior design before she transitioned to posting daily outfits. Her fashionable yet effortless looks gained Internet fame. Since, she has become one of the Business of Fashion's (BoF) 500 most influential people in the fashion industry; served as a brand ambassador for Chloé, Giorgio Armani Beauty, and Dior, among others; been on Forbes' 30 Under 30; and authored her *New York Times* best-seller, *Capture Your Style*. Despite her fame, Aimee remains down-to-earth and loves sharing stories on her blog and YouTube channel.

KOREAN JAPANESE AMERICAN FASHION BLOGGER

CONSTANCE WU
1982

Constance Tianming Wu was born on March 22, 1982 to Taiwanese immigrant parents in Richmond, Virginia. She was a founding supporter of Time's Up and is vocal about prejudice in Hollywood's entertainment industry. She stars in *Fresh Off the Boat*, an American sitcom set in 90's Florida, and the first sitcom starring an Asian American family since Margaret Cho's *All-American Girl* in 1994. She also starred in *Crazy Rich Asians*, a romantic comedy-drama based on the novel by Singaporean American Kevin Kwan, and the first all-Asian film cast since *The Joy Luck Club* in 1993. As of writing this book, Constance has been nominated for a Golden Globe!

TAIWANESE AMERICAN ACTRESS

Before CRAZY RICH ASIANS,
I hadn't even done a tiny part in a studio film.
I never dreamed I would get to star in one...

because I had never seen that happen to someone who looked **like me**

—CONSTANCE WU

TAM TRAN
1982

Tam Tran was born in Germany on October 30, 1982. After the Fall of Saigon in 1975, her parents became *boat people*, Vietnamese refugees who escaped the Vietnam War by boat. Her parents were rescued by the German navy. In Germany, they gave birth to Tam and her younger brother, Thien. When Tam was six, her family moved to the United States. She grew up in Garden Grove, California where she excelled at school. To save money, she attended Santa Ana Community College, and in 2003, Tam was accepted as a transfer student to UCLA. However, Tam feared that she could not go to UCLA because her family could not afford tuition. She would have applied for financial aid, but Tam had a secret... Tam was undocumented.

UNDOCUMENTED VIETNAMESE AMERICAN
ACTIVIST, SCHOLAR

The Tran family had applied for political asylum immediately after arriving the United States. But, after years of waiting, their request was denied. They became *undocumented* meaning they were not considered legal residents of the United States and could be deported. Where would they go? Germany does not grant citizenship to children born there, so Tam could not live in Germany. Vietnam was the country the Trans had fled, so she did not belong there either. Tam was stateless; according to law, she had no home.

While a full-time UCLA student who worked multiple jobs, Tam used her free time to fight for fellow undocumented students. Tam was also a gifted filmmaker and produced two documentaries to share her and her friends' stories.

I hate filling out forms...
PLACE OF BIRTH: GERMANY ←
(But I'm not German.)
ETHNICITY: VIETNAMESE ←
(But I've never been to Vietnam.)

These forms never ask where I was raised and educated.

I was born in GERMANY, my parents are VIETNAMESE, but I have been AMERICAN raised & educated for 18 years.

On May 18, 2007, Tam bravely testified before Congress to tell her story. Three days later, ICE (Immigration and Customs Enforcement) agents arrested her parents and younger brother at her home. Luckily, Tam reached out to her allies in Congress and freed her family.

35

Tam was one of the few undocumented students to attend Graduate School. She was accepted into Brown University's American Civilization PhD Program. Tam, always light-hearted, joked, "Maybe if I get a PhD in American Civilization, they will finally let me become an American!" Before Tam could become a legal citizen, she and her close friend and fellow undocumented activist, Cinthya Felix, were killed in a car accident by a drunk driver. Though they lived such short lives, they made a profound impact on the lives of many fellow undocumented students, allies, and the next generation.

ANNA AKANA

1989

STAY AWESOME GOTHAM!

Anna Kay Akana was born on August 18, 1989. On Valentine's Day 2007, Anna's 13-year-old sister, Kristina, died by suicide. Anna could not laugh for months until she saw Margaret Cho perform on Comedy Central.

Since, she has used comedy and laughter as way to heal and help others find joy in their lives despite hardships and sadness. Anna's YouTube channel, where she posts comedy skits and short films, has over 2 million subscribers.

JAPANESE, FILIPINO, HAWAIIAN, IRISH, GERMAN, SPANISH, ENGLISH AMERICAN

ACTRESS, COMEDIAN, YOUTUBER

TERISA SIAGATONU
1988

Born in 1988 in San Francisco, California, Terisa identifies as a queer Samoan woman. A poet and educator, she has performed at the White House during the Obama administration and the UN Conference on Climate Change in Paris, France. In 2012, she received President Obama's Champion of Change Award for her activism as a spoken word poet/organizer in her Pacific Islander Community. She continues to create works and educate others about educational attainment, Pacific Islander and Indigenous rights, climate change, the LGBTQQIA community, mental health and healing, and more.

SAMOAN AMERICAN
SPOKEN WORD POET, ORGANIZER,
THERAPIST, EDUCATOR

AMANDA PHINGBODHIPAKKIYA
1989

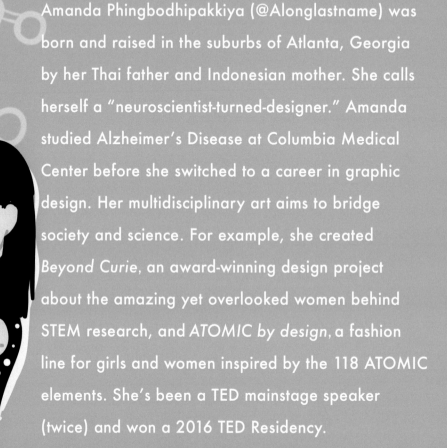

Amanda Phingbodhipakkiya (@Alonglastname) was born and raised in the suburbs of Atlanta, Georgia by her Thai father and Indonesian mother. She calls herself a "neuroscientist-turned-designer." Amanda studied Alzheimer's Disease at Columbia Medical Center before she switched to a career in graphic design. Her multidisciplinary art aims to bridge society and science. For example, she created *Beyond Curie*, an award-winning design project about the amazing yet overlooked women behind STEM research, and *ATOMIC by design*, a fashion line for girls and women inspired by the 118 ATOMIC elements. She's been a TED mainstage speaker (twice) and won a 2016 TED Residency.

I WANTED TO SHARE THE RICH HISTORY OF WOMEN DRIVING SOCIETY FORWARD WITH THE NEXT GENERATION

THAI INDONESIAN AMERICAN
ARTIST, CREATIVE DIRECTOR, NEUROSCIENTIST

FATIMAH ASGHAR
1990

Fatimah (her friends call her "Fati") is a child of immigrants who escaped Kashmir during the violence between India and Pakistan. Her parents died when she was a child, and she was raised by a new immigrant family in Cambridge, Massachusetts. She wrote and co-created *Brown Girls*, an Emmy-nominated web series about the friendship between two women of color: Leila, a South Asian American, queer writer and Patricia, a Black American musician. She has also published her poetry book *If They Should Come for Us* and a chapter-book *After*, and in 2017, she was a recipient of the Ruth Lilly and Dorothy Sargent Rosenberg Poetry Fellowship from the Poetry Foundation.

PAKISTANI KASHMIRI MUSLIM AMERICAN
POET, SCREEN WRITER, EDUCATOR, PERFORMER

MITSKI
1990

Mitski Miyawaki was born on September 27, 1990 in Japan to a white American father and Japanese mother, and grew up in New York City. Mitski did not grow up with musical instruments. Nevertheless, she learned to create music by "writing things down on paper, hearing it in her head, and hoping for the best." She studied studio compositions at Purchase College's Conservatory of Music, and during that time, self-released her first two albums. Since, she's continued producing indie-rock jams including her lead single, *Your Best American Girl*, which tackles the complexities of her Asian American identity. Mitski is *hapa*, a Native Hawaiian word that literally means "port" or "mix," but today, often refers to anyone of mixed Asian heritage. Mitski feels "half Japanese, half American but not fully either."

JAPANESE WHITE AMERICAN SINGER, MUSICIAN

your best
American Girl

HAYLEY KIYOKO

Hayley Kiyoko Alcroft was born April 3, 1991 in Los Angeles, California to a Japanese Canadian mother and European American father. After a career as a child actress, performing for Nickelodeon and Disney Channel, even staring in the Disney Channel movie *Lemonade Mouth*, Haley began a successful career as a musician.

Hayley knew she was attracted to girls when she was six, and came out to accepting parents in the sixth grade. She is openly gay and hopes to normalize lesbian relationships in society through her music.

JAPANESE WHITE AMERICAN SINGER, MUSICIAN

AC DUMLAO
1991

Mx. AC Dumlao was born on December 17, 1991 and grew up in Long Island, New York. AC is a queer non-binary first generation Filipinx American child of immigrants, and uses they/them pronouns. Unlike she/her or he/his, they/them pronouns are gender neutral. AC created the social justice news Facebook page "Call Me They" and the fashion and self-care Instagram @menswearselfcare. They also run the Name Change Project to help low-income transgender and non-binary folks legally change their names. "[I] hope by being visible, I can help others," AC told NBC News (Asian America #RedefineAtoZ, 2017).

FILIPINX AMERICAN
ADVOCATE, EDUCATOR, ARTIST

45

RUBY IBARRA
1993

Ruby Ibarra was born on February 25, 1993 in Tacloban, Philippines. At age 4, her family immigrated to San Lorenzo, California. Her life in the Bay Area exposed her to a variety of cultures, experiences, and most importantly, hip hop. She grew up as a 90's kid blasting Tupac, Eminem, and Wu Tang Clan. After graduating from UC Davis, she began her career as a singer, songwriter, and music producer. She started posting on Youtube in 2010, and since has had three independent videos each gain over a million views in less than a week. Rapping in both Tagalog and English, she hopes to express the significance of Filipino culture on her identity.

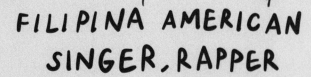

FILIPINA AMERICAN
SINGER, RAPPER

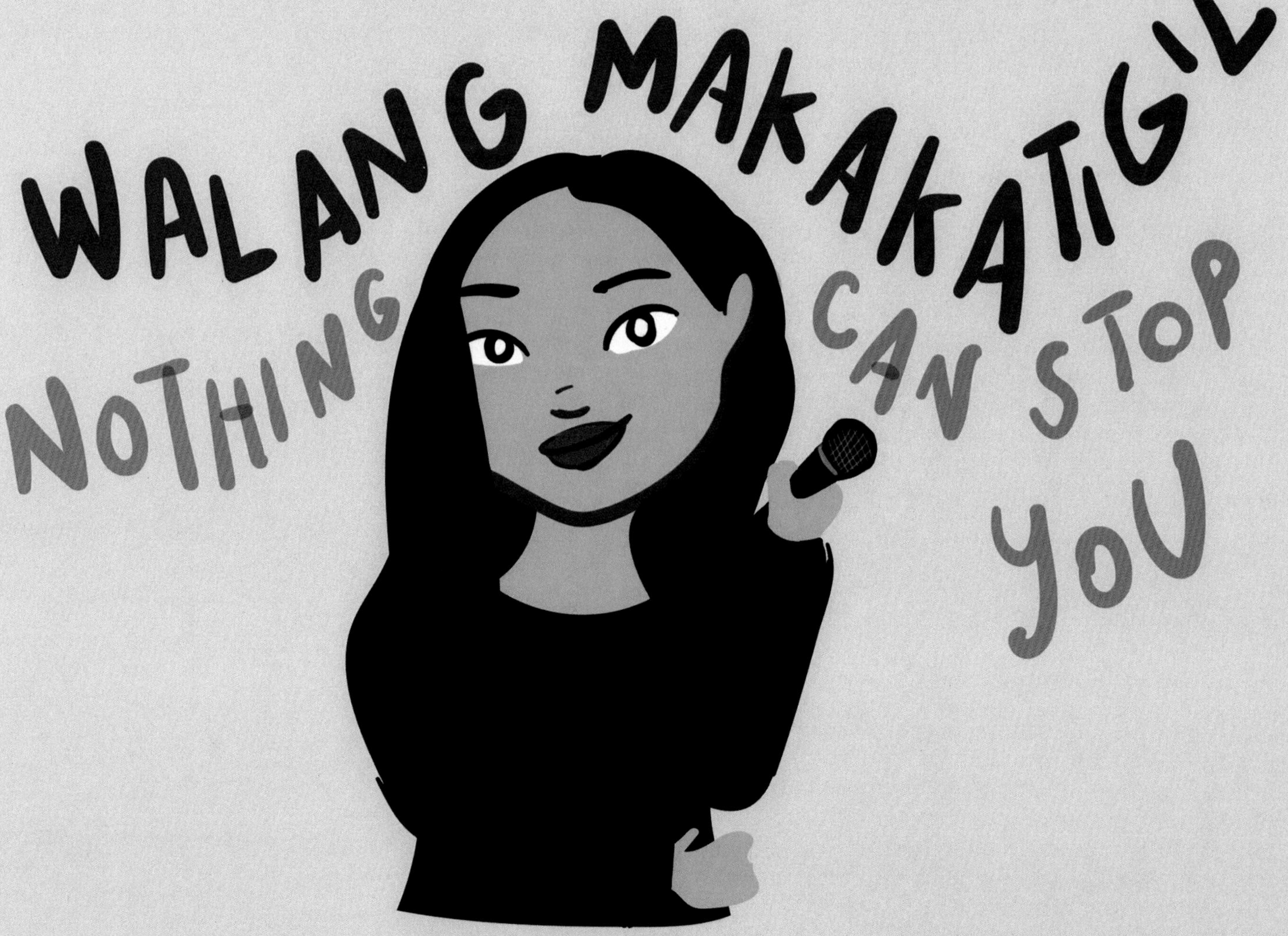
WALANG MAKAKATIGIL
NOTHING CAN STOP YOU

ANGEL TRAZO
1995

Talitha Angelica Acaylar Trazo was born on June 18, 1995 in San Jose, California to Filipino immigrant parents. When she was six, she knew that she wanted to become a "writer and illustrator" but was afraid that this dream was too risky. So, she was a Biology major and Pre-Med student at Colgate University. However, she continued to make art through her second major, Studio Art.

hiii

uwu

I drew this using photoshop + wacom tablet

teaspoon boba

UCLA

ucla

LIVE WELL

KNOW HISTORY KNOW SELF

B.B.B

To Do:

THANK YOU!
you are inspiring!

After graduating college in 2017, she didn't apply to Pre-Med post-baccalaureate programs as she'd planned. Instead, she took on a summer marketing internship in NYC. When that ended, she spent a year working retail and took her first Asian American Studies class at De Anza community college.

During this gap year, she realized her passion for ethnic studies and applied to graduate programs. She was admitted to UCLA as an Asian American Studies MA student and hopes to graduate in 2020. Angel dreams of becoming a historian and sharing stories through the visual arts.

angeltrazo.com
instagram @angeltrazo
twitter @angel_trazo

ACKNOWLEDGEMENTS

I started this project in August 2018. I was at the Recycle Bookstore in Campbell, searching for Asian American Studies books per usual. While browsing the children's section, I was inspired by the growing collection of books about women. However, I was looking for a particular kind of woman. Where were my Asian Americans at? So, I asked the bookstore clerk, "Are there any books like this one?" I gestured to the amazing *Little Leaders: Bold Women in Black History* by Vashti Harrison. "Except like," I continued, "About Asian Americans?"

"I... don't think so," he replied. This is where my project of making a book about Asian American women began.

In my obsessive state of artistic fervor, I created the first draft of stories and art in two weeks. Then, I went to grad school and put the project on hold. In October, I created a Kickstarer to help fund the first round of book prints and estimate pre-orders. My goal was $550. I reached my goal in 2 days, and by the end of the month, 67 kind humans had pledged $2,393. Now that it's winter break, I'm finally able to finish my last round of edits. And that's the tea.

A huge thank you to...

my family who has always supported my artistic endeavors.

the 67 folks who pledged to bring my first edition print to life through Kickstarter

Piper McNulty for helping edit the book's copy

the following friend groups: The Fearsome Five, SLAYSIANZ, LESBROZ, APALI (Asian Pacific American Leadership Institute), the folks at Hangar X, The Phamily, Love is an Open Door, my friends from Colgate University, Damaged Goods, Gudetama Poops, and my friends from the Asian American Studies Department & Asian American Studies Center at UCLA

my coworkers at the Nordstrom Rack who saw me start this project during my lunch breaks

my 360-ish Instagram followers for their edits and supportive feedback

the kind folks at JS Stew House (now, Bento Box in Milpitas), Teaspoon, BeiBay, Tea Lyfe, Fresh Roast, and Bon Bon Tea House who let me plant myself in their shops to work for hours at a time

— Angel Trazo, December 2018

selected WORKS CITED

for full list, please visit angeltrazo.com

Bennet, Cara. "Celebrating Asian American Women." *National Women's History Museum*, April 26, 2018. https://www.womenshistory.org/articles/celebrating-asian-american-women

NBC News. "NBC Asian America Presents: A to Z." www.nbcnews.com/atoz

Wong, Kent, Shadduck-Hernández, Janna, Inzunza, Fabiola, Monroe, Julie, Narro, Victor, and Abel Valenzuela Jr. (Eds.) Undocumented and Unafraid: Tam Tran, Cinthya Felix, and the Immigrant Youth Movement. Los Anglees, CA: UCLA Center for Labor Research and Education, 2012

Yoo, Paul and Lin Wang. Shining Star: The Anna May Wong Story. New York, NY: Lee & Low Books, 2008.

Zia, Helen. Asian American Dreams: The Emergence of an American People. New York, NY: Farrar, Straus and Giroux, 2000.